CHERYL MALKOWSKI

Blocks *to* Diamonds

KALEIDOSCOPE STAR QUILTS FROM TRADITIONAL BLOCKS

C&T PUBLISHING

Text copyright © 2010 by Cheryl Malkowski

Artwork copyright © 2010 by C&T Publishing, Inc.

PUBLISHER: Amy Marson

CREATIVE DIRECTOR: Gailen Runge

ACQUISITIONS EDITOR: Susanne Woods

EDITOR: Karla Menaugh

TECHNICAL EDITORS: Teresa Stroin and Janice Wray

COPYEDITOR/PROOFREADER: Wordfirm Inc.

COVER/BOOK DESIGNER: Kristen Yenche

PRODUCTION COORDINATOR: Jenny Leicester

PRODUCTION EDITOR: Alice Mace Nakanishi

ILLUSTRATORS: Kirstie Pettersen and Aliza Shalit

PHOTOGRAPHY by Christina Carty-Francis and Diane Pedersen of C&T Publishing, Inc., unless otherwise noted

Published by C&T Publishing, Inc., P.O. Box 1456, Lafayette, CA 94549

Library of Congress Cataloging-in-Publication Data

Malkowski, Cheryl, 1955-

Blocks to diamonds : kaleidoscope star quilts from traditional blocks / by Cheryl Malkowski.

    p. cm.

ISBN 978-1-57120-908-5 (soft cover)

1. Patchwork--Patterns. 2. Quilting--Patterns. I. Title.

TT835.M27174 2010

746.46'041--dc22

                        2009054001

Printed in China

10 9 8 7 6 5 4 3 2 1

Appreciation

This book would not have been written without the help of the ladies from the Umpqua Valley (Oregon) Quilters Guild, students, and quilting friends. Once again, they have volunteered to be my testers and quiltmakers and have made some spectacular quilts in the process. I'd especially like to thank Barb Watson, who introduced me to paperless paper piecing, and Ramonda Weckerle, who showed me the cool pinning trick presented in this book.

It has again been my pleasure to work with the staff at C&T, who were full of ideas and always helpful. I can't imagine a more perfect group of people with whom to make a book.

I don't even know how my husband puts up with me. We have always said he is the one who works too much, but he has persevered with me through this one, and I am grateful. Thank you, Tom!

Bosco the dog hasn't done a single, solitary thing to help me with this book except to supply distraction often enough that my body didn't actually freeze in the typing/sewing position. I guess he does what he can.

Contents

INTRODUCTION. **4**

GENERAL PIECING INSTRUCTIONS . . . **5**

BLOCKS-TO-DIAMONDS PROJECTS . . **14**

    Annie's Choice block:
    Raspberry Sunflowers. **14**

    Flying Geese block:
    My Gaggle of Geese **17**
    Whirlwind Romance **20**

    Striped Flying Geese block:
    Flamenco Dancer **23**

    Joseph's Coat block:
    Desert Flower. **26**

    New York Beauty block:
    Baja Sunrise. **30**

    Optical Illusion block:
    Wintermint **34**

    Rolling Squares block:
    Radiant Jewels **37**

    Steps to the Altar block:
    Tropical Vista. **40**

    Storm at Sea block:
    Tuscan Star **43**

    Summer Winds block:
    Frost on the Window **46**

    Woven Logs block:
    Solar Flare. **52**

GALLERY **57**

RESOURCES **64**

ABOUT THE AUTHOR **64**

Introduction

There are some designs that every quilter seems to make at least once in her, or his, quilting career. The traditional Radiant Star is one of them. I had always admired the way colors can be placed within the design to make it glow or contrast, as well as all the room the design has for beautiful quilting, but I had never actually put one together. So how could I resist joining a group of my friends who were all working on such a project? I couldn't.

The prospect of a new project had my wheels turning, but when it came right down to buying the fabric for the quilt, I couldn't bring myself to do it. I just couldn't stand the idea of making the same quilt as everyone else, even if my colors were different.

So I went into my studio to see what could satisfy my longing to have one of these beauties without it being the same thing. The result was this series of quilts that skew a traditional block into a diamond to form one arm of the star. From there I also added designs that put the skewed blocks into different traditional settings.

Paper piecing was the likely technique to get these oddly shaped pieces together. But I'm a girl who won't sew anything that doesn't require power tools—and picking out all that paper sounded a lot like handwork to me. So I've provided you with foundation patterns for most designs and given instructions for a paperless paper-piecing technique. Using this technique, along with a clever method for matching seams between blocks, makes these quilts go together accurately with a minimum of extra fuss. Maybe it's time for you to make your masterpiece!

General Piecing Instructions

Getting Started

All you need to get started turning blocks to diamonds is a basic quilting tool kit with a few extras. You'll need some very fine, sharp pins; a dull or old sewing machine needle (so you don't ruin a new one when sewing through freezer paper); a Sharpie; paper scissors; and an Add-A-Quarter ruler (see Resources, page 64).

Preparing the Pattern

1. Cut the pattern out, leaving enough room to apply staples around the edges, ½" or so. This is your master pattern.

2. Cut 8 pieces of freezer paper large enough to place the pattern on.

3. Stack the 8 pieces of freezer paper, *shiny side up*, and lay the pattern faceup on top. Staple around the edges of the pattern (about ½" outside the dashed line) to hold the freezer paper in place.

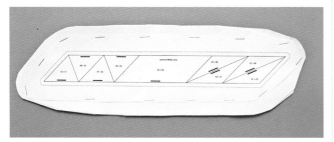

Staple freezer paper (shiny side up) to master pattern.

4. Using a dull sewing machine needle without thread, stitch on all the solid (stitching) lines of the pattern, going through the pattern and all the thicknesses of freezer paper. Use a short stitch length to make the perforations fold easily later on.

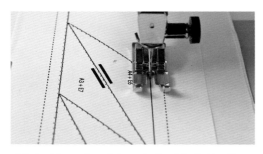

Stitch without thread through all solid stitching lines.

5. Cut out the pattern along the dotted outside line, through all the freezer-paper layers. These pieces of freezer paper are your working templates.

6. Use a narrow felt marker, such as a Sharpie, to label either the master or your individual templates on the matte side of the freezer paper with the name of the piece (A1, A2, and so on). Also label the position of the strip placement line in each piece, the color that each piece is going to be, and the width of the fabric strip to use. The Sharpie will show through the freezer paper a little bit and help with positioning the fabric.

> **tip** Labeling correctly could be a little tricky because now the matte side of the freezer-paper templates is the mirror image of the master pattern. Carefully label the matte side of the freezer paper, keeping that in mind. Labeling the wrong side of the master pattern first, which has the printing already on the front of it, and then copying from that is an alternative that will make this easier.

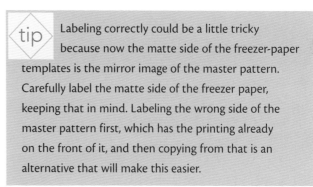

Strip placement lines

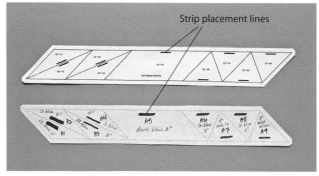

Use Sharpie to mark numbers and lines on matte side of freezer paper. Remember that this is a mirror image!

Paperless Paper Piecing

In each unit, stitch the pieces together in numerical order, starting with 1 and continuing until the last piece is attached.

1. Press the wrong side of the fabric strip for piece A1 to the shiny side of the unit A freezer-paper template, making sure that A1 is completely covered, with at least ¼" around the edges for seam allowances, and that the strip placement line is parallel to the straight-grain cut edge of the fabric strip.

> **tip** For best cutting results, use a separate fabric strip for each piece and alternate alignment from one side of the strip to the other each time. This will help the pieces nest together when you're cutting and will use less fabric.
>
>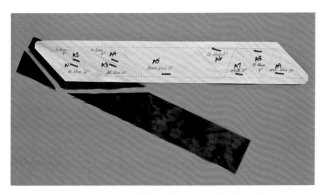
>
> Save fabric by alternating sides of strip for pieces.

2. Cut away excess strip fabric from the outside of the paper, close to the paper's edge and at the same angle as the paper.

Cut away excess strip fabric from outside edge of paper.

3. Fold back at the perforated line along the seam you are about to sew—the seam between pieces A1 and A2. Trim the seam allowance of A1 to ¼" using an Add-A-Quarter ruler.

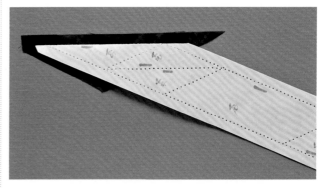

Fold back at perforation and trim seam allowance.

4. Check the strip placement line for A2 and place the fabric strip for piece A2 under piece A1, right sides together, with the straight-grain cut edge of the fabric strip parallel to the strip placement line. Also, make sure that the fabric strip is placed so that all of piece A2 will be covered. This may mean shifting the fabric strip back and forth along the raw edge so that it is positioned correctly and parallel to the strip placement line.

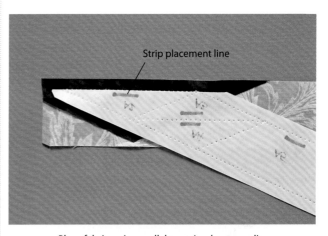

Strip placement line

Place fabric strip parallel to strip placement line.

> **tip** You can see whether the new piece of fabric will cover the pattern by holding it up and checking. The new pattern piece is folded to the front, so look behind it to see whether the new fabric covers the whole area. Remember to align with the strip placement line!

5. Stitch together right next to the folded freezer paper, going 2 to 3 stitches past the edges at the beginning and the end of the section.

Stitch next to folded freezer paper.

Closeup of stitching line, just next to folded freezer paper

6. Unfold the freezer paper and place it on the pressing surface with the fabric side up. Press to make a very crisp, precise seam.

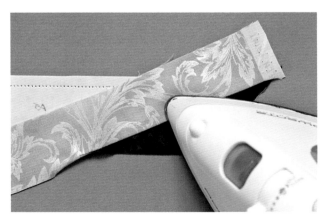

Press with fabric side up.

> **tip** Accurate pressing is vital! If you don't press with care, all the extra work you put into paper piecing is wasted! So get the tip of your iron right next to the seam and run it along the whole length of the seam, nudging the fabric over onto the seam allowance of the fabric you just stitched onto the unit.

7. Trim away the end of the fabric strip close to the paper's edge and at the same angle as the paper.

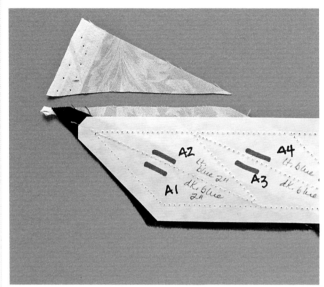

Cut away excess strip fabric next to outer edge of paper.

8. Fold back the paper at the next seamline.

Fold back paper at next seamline.

9. Use the Add-A-Quarter ruler to trim the seam allowance ¼" from the fold.

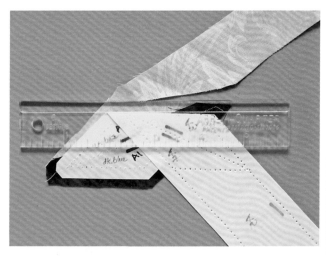

Use Add-A-Quarter ruler to trim seam allowance.

tip   Many of the patterns presented in this book use very long, oddly shaped triangles. I have found that if you follow Step 9 above, rather than randomly cutting off a rectangle at the end of a long triangle, a significant amount of fabric can be saved by then placing the pattern on the opposite side of the strip for the next cut. The strips are sized so that there is room to do this, with some breathing space between the triangles. If you want to be able to whack away after every piece randomly, I recommend purchasing at least ⅛ to ¼ yard of extra fabric in each color.

10. Align and place the new fabric strip, as described in Step 4 (page 6). Stitch next to the folded freezer paper.

11. Continue in the same manner all around each unit, following the numbering schematic and pressing, then trimming, after each new fabric piece is added.

WATCHING OUT FOR THE STRIP PLACEMENT LINE

Notice that each pattern piece has a thick black line next to one of the seamlines. This is the strip placement line. It's very important to line up *that* edge of the pattern piece (or one parallel to it) with the original straight-grain cut edge of the fabric strip. This will ensure that the piece will fit on the fabric strip and that you will make the most of your fabric.

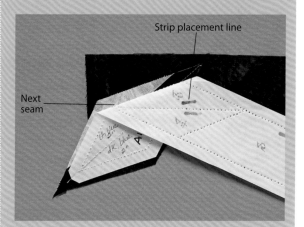

Sometimes the strip placement line is not along the next seam to be sewn. Line it up with the straight-grain cut edge of the fabric strip anyway.

Sew the next seam, then trim away the excess seam allowance ¼" from the paper with an Add-A-Quarter ruler.

12. When all the pieces are on the unit, use scissors or a rotary cutter to cut out along the dashed outer line.

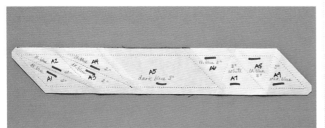

Trimmed unit, front and back view

> **tip** An alternate method of cutting is to determine the shape needed for each piece of the unit, cut all the pieces at once, and use the precut shapes, instead of strips, to piece the units.
>
> To determine the shape of each piece, place the fabric strip under the folded freezer paper as in Step 4 (page 6), but do not stitch yet. Fold back the freezer paper along each adjoining seamline and trim the fabric ¼" away from each fold, using the Add-A-Quarter ruler. Use this piece as your template, adding a bit of extra fabric around the edges, and cut as many as you need for your project.

Piecing the Units into Diamond Blocks

Note: If the diamond block is made from only one unit, use these instructions to help piece the blocks into a star.

1. Gently remove the freezer paper from the units that form the blocks. Mark the ¼" seam allowances with dots on the corners of the units on the wrong side of the fabric.

Gently remove freezer paper from fabric.

> **tips** ◆ Whenever possible, remove the freezer paper, beginning with piece number 1 on the unit. This will help keep the seams from coming unsewn in this step.
>
> ◆ If your project has been allowed to age with the freezer paper attached, or if the fabric is clinging tightly to the freezer paper, press to rewarm the adhesive. It should come right off!

2. Push a pin straight through the corner marks and seam allowance intersections of both layers of the units where you will be stitching. Once the pin is straight through both layers, slant it and put it all the way in.

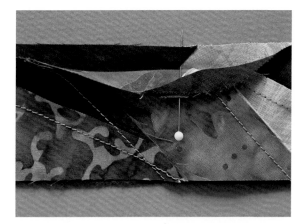

Pin through both intersections.

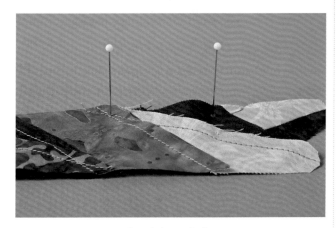

Stand pin vertically.

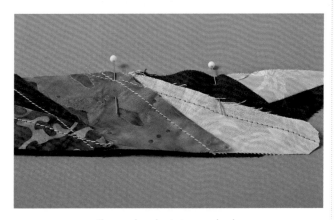

Slant and push pin in completely.

tip I've attempted to make all the seam allowances nest together nicely, but sometimes that's not possible with this technique. You may find that you need to clip and press or nudge a seam allowance in a different direction to get the seams to nest.

3. Stitch from raw edge to raw edge, *bringing each pin back up to a vertical position* about 1" before you get to it. Let the pin ride slowly toward the needle until it is almost under it. Remove the pin and continue stitching.

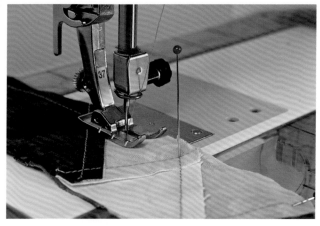

Return pin to vertical position without removing.

Let pin ride slowly toward needle.

4. For the gentle curves in some patterns, follow Steps 1–3, then just be sure both of the raw edges are together while stitching.

Adding Background

1. For background squares, mark the ¼" seam allowances with dots at the corners of the diamond blocks on the wrong side of the fabric. Measure from one corner dot to the next corner dot on several blocks to determine the average distance. The measurements should be very close.

2. Add ½" to the average measurement and cut 4 square blocks that size.

3. Mark the ¼" seam allowances at the corners of the squares. For a 50" star, these squares should measure approximately 15¼" × 15¼".

4. Set up the diamond blocks, squares, and side setting triangles on a design wall or surface.

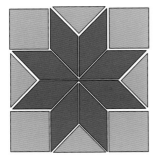

Lay out quilt.

5. Find a place where the background square and a diamond block are to be stitched together. Place the diamond block on top of the background square, right sides together, matching the marks at the corners. Pin.

6. Stitch together from the inside corner mark to the outside raw edge, leaving the inner ends open.

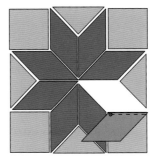

Stitch from center dot to outer edge.

7. Choose another diamond block that is adjacent to the same background square (it will be sewn at a 90° angle to the first seam). Repeat Steps 5 and 6.

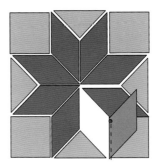

Place adjacent diamond block on top of background square; stitch.

8. Stitch together the 2 diamond blocks, using the same method used to piece the units together, and stopping ¼" from the corners at the marks. Make 4 units like this.

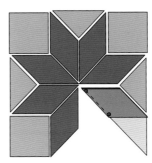

Stitch block to block.

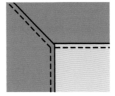

Intersection of 3 seams

9. Stitch a side setting triangle to one of the units from Step 8 by starting at the center mark and stitching toward the outside of the quilt. *Don't worry if the units don't end in the same place. The triangles are made purposely large so you will have enough to trim when you are finished, preserving the ¼" seam allowance.*

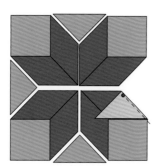

Add side setting triangle.

10. Stitch another unit from Step 8 to the other short side of the triangle and then stitch the diamond blocks together. Make 2.

11. Stitch 1 of the remaining side setting triangles to each of the units made in Step 10. Using the same methods as before, stitch the remaining seams, leaving the ends open until the very last seam that puts the star together. Press toward the background.

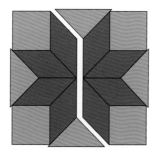

Quilt sections

tip You may want to stop stitching 4"–5" from the very center of the star on both sides of this last seam. Then you can baste it together to ensure that the center meets precisely as it should when you finish stitching.

12. Square up the quilt by placing a long ruler along each edge of the quilt. Align the ruler's edge along the raw edges of 2 corner squares and be sure to leave ¼" seam allowance outside the star points. The radiant stars in the project chapters should measure approximately 50½" × 50½" after being pieced together and trimmed.

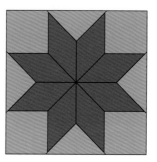

Square up quilt, leaving ¼" seam allowance outside star points.

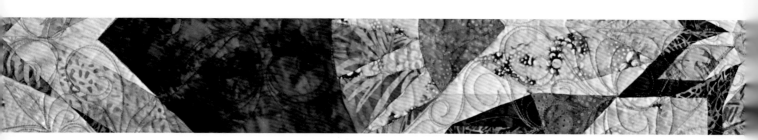

Alternate Settings

1. When putting the diamond blocks into other settings, such as the Rolling Star or the Carpenter's Wheel, follow the general directions in Adding a Background (page 11).

2. Mark the corners and stitch to the marks for all the seams that don't extend to the outside edges of the quilt top.

3. Complete the remaining seams by stitching all the way to the outside edges.

4. Use the diagrams below as a guide for grouping the blocks.

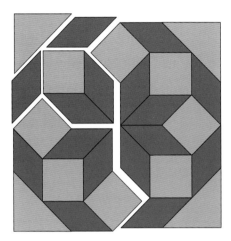

Rolling Star setting

Carpenter's Wheel setting

Adding Borders

All the plain borders in this book are stitched the same way.

1. If required, piece the border strips together end to end with diagonal seams. Press the seam allowances to one side.

2. Cut the strips into the lengths indicated in the instructions. There will be 2 shorter strips and 2 longer strips. If you prefer, you can measure your quilt and adapt the border lengths to fit its measurements.

3. Stitch the short strips to the top and bottom of the quilt and the long strips to the sides. Press toward the borders. Repeat with additional borders as required.

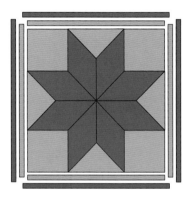

Add borders.

ANNIE'S CHOICE BLOCK

Raspberry Sunflowers

65″ × 65″, by Jane Yurk, quilted by Richard Weckerle, 2009

◆ SKILL LEVEL: **Confident Beginner**

The colors in this diamond block are arranged to make a small star inside the larger one. With only two shapes, construction is very simple. Look at *Blueberries* by Kathy Thompson (page 59) to see another setting and a different scheme for color placement.

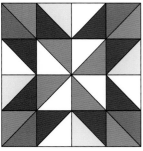

Annie's Choice square block   Annie's Choice diamond block

Fabric Requirements
and Cutting Instructions

All requirements are based on 40" usable width of fabric. See General Piecing
Instructions (page 5) for details on cutting methods as needed.

YARDAGE	FOR	CUTTING
2 yards cream	A1	Cut 2 strips 2¼" wide.
	A5, C1	Cut 2 strips 3½" wide.
	After cutting the above strips, remove the selvage from one edge of the remaining large piece and make a lengthwise cut 9" from that edge.	
	Border 1 (narrow background border)	From the 9"-wide piece, cut 2 strips 2" × 50½" and 2 strips 2" × 53½".*
	Setting squares and triangles	From the remaining 31"-wide piece, cut 4 squares 15¼" × 15¼" and 1 square 23" × 23". Cut the 23" square twice diagonally to yield 4 triangles.
1⅝ yards sunflower print	C8, D4	Cut 3 strips 2¼" wide.
	B3, C4	Cut 2 strips 3½" wide.
	Border 3 (wide border)	Cut 7 strips 5½" wide. Piece 2 strips 5½" × 55½" and 2 strips 5½" × 65½".*
½ yard pale print	A2	Cut 2 strips 2¼" wide.
	B4, C3	Cut 2 strips 3½" wide.
⅜ yard green print	A6, B2, C2, D6	Cut 3 strips 3½" wide.
1½ yards fuchsia	A4, B5, B8, C7, D3	Cut 6 strips 2¼" wide.
	B1, D5	Cut 2 strips 3½" wide.
	Border 2 (narrow border)	Cut 6 strips 1½" wide. Piece 2 strips 1½" × 53½" and 2 strips 1½" × 55½".*
	Double-fold binding	Cut 8 strips 2¼" wide.

*Measure your finished quilt top and adjust the border lengths as needed. These measurements
are for a quilt top that measures 50½" × 50½" before borders.*

Continued on page 16

Continued from page 15

YARDAGE	FOR	CUTTING
⅝ yard pink	B6, C6, D2	Cut 4 strips 2¼″ wide.
	A7, D8	Cut 2 strips 3½″ wide.
⅝ yard green	A3, B7, C5, D1	Cut 5 strips 2¼″ wide.
	A8, D7	Cut 2 strips 3½″ wide.
2⅛ yards 108″-wide fabric	Backing	
Batting: 73″ × 73″		

Block Assembly

1. Use the Annie's Choice unit pattern (pattern pullout page P4) to make 8 freezer-paper templates of each unit. For this pattern, only 1 template is used for all 4 units in the diamond block, so you will need to print 4 copies of the template and label each copy with the letters and numbers for that unit. Note that for units A and D, the numbering starts on the end with the long, skinny triangles. For units B and C, the numbering starts on the opposite end.

2. Use the block map as a guide for color placement and to stitch the units into a diamond. Press the seam allowances toward row A. Make 8 diamonds.

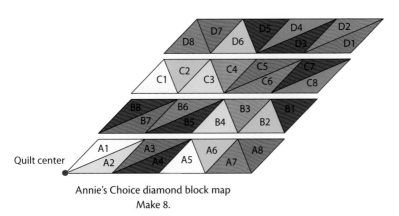

Quilt center

Annie's Choice diamond block map
Make 8.

Quilt Assembly

Follow the directions in General Piecing Instructions (page 5) to assemble the star and background and to add border strips.

FLYING GEESE BLOCK

My Gaggle of Geese

65″ × 65″, by Barbara Watson, quilted by Richard Weckerle, 2009

◆ SKILL LEVEL: **Confident Beginner**

This is the only design in the book where you stitch through the layers of freezer paper matte side up. When you put the shiny side of the freezer paper up and play with color placement a little, it yields the design in *Like the Wind* (page 60).

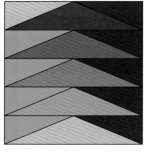

Flying Geese square block

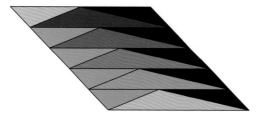

Flying Geese diamond block

Fabric Requirements and Cutting Instructions

All requirements are based on 40" usable width of fabric. See General Piecing Instructions (page 5) for details on cutting methods as needed.

YARDAGE	FOR	CUTTING
⅔ yard gold	A2, A5, A8, A11	Cut 7 strips 3" wide.
1⅝ yards cream	*Remove the selvage from one edge of the fabric and make a lengthwise cut 9" from that edge.*	
	Border 1 (narrow background border)	From the 9"-wide piece, cut 2 strips 2" × 50½" and 2 strips 2" × 53½".*
	Setting squares and triangles	From the remaining 31"-wide piece, cut 4 squares 15¼" × 15¼" and 1 square 23" × 23". Cut the 23" square twice diagonally to yield 4 triangles.
½ yard pale green	A1, A14	Cut 5 strips 3" wide.
⅓ yard light green	A4	Cut 3 strips 3" wide.
⅓ yard medium green	A7	Cut 3 strips 3" wide.
⅓ yard medium-dark green	A10	Cut 3 strips 3" wide.
⅓ yard dark green	A13	Cut 3 strips 3" wide.
1⅛ yards brown	A3, A6, A9, A12, A15	Cut 10 strips 2½" wide.
	Border 2 (contrasting narrow inside border)	Cut 6 strips 1½" wide. Piece 2 strips 1½" × 53½" and 2 strips 1½" × 55½".*
1¼ yards brown print	Border 3 (outer border)	Cut 7 strips 5½" wide. Piece 2 strips 5½" × 55½" and 2 strips 5½" × 65½".*
2⅛ yards 108"-wide fabric	Backing	

Batting: 73" × 73"

Measure your finished quilt top and adjust the border lengths as needed. These measurements are for a quilt top that measures 50½" × 50½" before borders.

Block Assembly

1. Use the Flying Geese diamond block pattern (pattern pullout page P4) to make 8 freezer-paper templates of the block. It's very important—for this quilt only—to put the freezer paper *matte side up* when stitching the pattern to make the templates. If you don't, you'll end up with templates that make the quilt *Like the Wind* (page 60). Ask me how I know!

2. Use the block map as a guide for color placement. Make 8 diamonds.

Quilt center

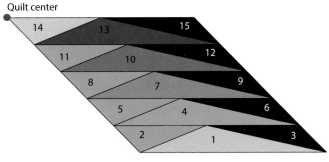

Flying Geese diamond block map
Make 8.

Quilt Assembly

Follow the directions in General Piecing Instructions (page 5) to assemble the star and background and to add border strips.

FLYING GEESE BLOCK

Whirlwind Romance

71″ × 71″, by Ronald D. Riley, 2009

◆ SKILL LEVEL: Skilled Beginner

I love the movement in this pattern! It uses a combination of diamond and square blocks in a Rolling Star setting. Look at *Swirling Water* by Pat Glass (page 58), where she turned the square blocks differently for another effect. For a look at a single-star version of this quilt, see *Like the Wind* (page 60); refer to the fabric requirements and cutting instructions in the chart on page 22.

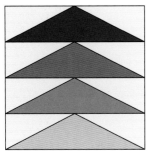

Flying Geese square block   Flying Geese diamond block

Fabric Requirements and Cutting Instructions

All requirements are based on 40" usable width of fabric. See General Piecing Instructions (page 5) for details on cutting methods as needed.

YARDAGE	FOR	CUTTING
Note: Purples 1–6 start with a very pale purple (1) and gradate to a dark purple (6).		
¾ yard purple 1	A4	Cut 3 strips 3" wide.
	B4	Cut 3 strips 4" wide.
¾ yard purple 2	A7	Cut 3 strips 3" wide.
	B7	Cut 3 strips 4" wide.
⅞ yard purple 3	A10	Cut 3 strips 3" wide.
	B10	Cut 3 strips 4" wide.
	C4	Cut 1 strip 5" wide.
⅞ yard purple 4	A13	Cut 3 strips 3" wide.
	B13	Cut 3 strips 4" wide.
	C1	Cut 1 strip 5" wide.
⅞ yard purple 5	A1	Cut 3 strips 3" wide.
	B1	Cut 3 strips 4" wide.
	C7	Cut 1 strip 5" wide.
2⅞ yards purple 6	A2, A5, A8, A11, A14	Cut 8 strips 3" wide.
	B2, B5, B8, B11, B14	Cut 6 strips 4" wide.
	C2, C3, C5, C6, C8, C9	Cut 9 strips 3½" wide.
	Double-fold binding	Cut 8 strips 2¼" wide.
3 yards light green	A3, A6, A9, A12, A15	Cut 10 strips 2½" wide.
	B3, B6, B9, B12, B15	Cut 6 strips 4" wide.
	Background	Cut 8 diamonds the size of the template for the pieced diamond block.
	C10	Cut 1 strip 5" wide.
2¼ yards 108"-wide fabric	Backing	

Batting: 79" × 79"

Block Assembly

1. Use the Flying Geese diamond block, square block, and corner triangle block patterns (pattern pullout pages P1, P2, and P4) to make 8 freezer-paper templates each of the diamond and square blocks and 4 of the corner triangle block.

2. Use the block maps as guides for color placement. The numbering follows the same pattern in the square and diamond blocks.

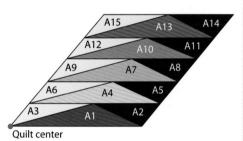

Flying Geese diamond block map
Make 8.

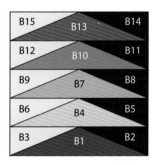

Flying Geese square block map
Make 8.

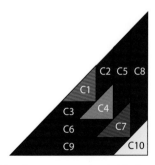

Flying Geese corner triangle block map
Make 4.

Quilt Assembly

Follow the directions in General Piecing Instructions (page 5) to assemble the star and background. Refer to the diagram for the Rolling Star setting (page 13).

• QUILT VARIATION •

Single-Star Version: Flying Geese

This version can be seen in Like the Wind *(page 60).*

The following fabric requirements and cutting instructions are for a 53″ × 53″ quilt. All requirements are based on 40″ usable width of fabric. See General Piecing Instructions (page 5) for details on cutting methods as needed.

YARDAGE	FOR	CUTTING
Note: Purples 1–6 start with a very pale purple (1) and gradate to a dark purple (6), in this example.		
⅜ yard purple 1	A4	Cut 3 strips 3″ wide.
⅜ yard purple 2	A7	Cut 3 strips 3″ wide.
⅜ yard purple 3	A10	Cut 3 strips 3″ wide.
⅜ yard purple 4	A13	Cut 3 strips 3″ wide.
⅜ yard purple 5	A1	Cut 3 strips 3″ wide.
1¼ yards purple 6	A2, A5, A8, A11, A14	Cut 8 strips 3″ wide.
	Double-fold binding	Cut 7 strips 2¼″ wide.
2⅓ yards light green	A3, A6, A9, A12, A15	Cut 10 strips 2½″ wide.
	After cutting the above strips, remove the selvage from one edge of the remaining large piece and make a lengthwise cut 9″ from that edge.	
	Narrow background border	From the 9″-wide piece, cut 2 strips 2″ × 50½″ and 2 strips 2″ × 53½″.*
	Background squares and triangles	From the remaining 31″-wide piece, cut 4 squares 15¼″ × 15¼″ and 1 square 23″ × 23″. Cut the 23″ square twice diagonally to yield 4 triangles.
1¾ yards 108″-wide fabric	Backing	
Batting: 61″ × 61″		

*Measure your finished quilt top and adjust the border lengths as needed. These measurements are for a quilt top that measures 50½″ × 50½″ before borders.

STRIPED FLYING GEESE BLOCK

Flamenco Dancer

86″ × 86″, by Cheryl Malkowski, 2009

◆ **SKILL LEVEL: Intermediate**

Use strip sets, instead of paper piecing, to piece half this block!

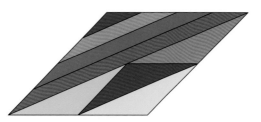

Striped Flying Geese square block   Striped Flying Geese diamond block

Fabric Requirements and Cutting Instructions

All requirements are based on 40" usable width of fabric. See General Piecing Instructions (page 5) for details on cutting methods as needed.

YARDAGE	FOR	CUTTING
⅔ yard pale green	A1, B1	Cut 7 strips 3" wide.
1 yard fuchsia	A2	Cut 4 strips 3" wide.
	Strip sets for striped diamond halves	Cut 11 strips 1½" wide.
1⅛ yards orange	A3, B3	Cut 7 strips 3" wide.
	Border 2 (narrow contrasting border)	Cut 8 strips 1½" wide. Piece 2 strips 1½" × 72½" and 2 strips 1½" × 74½".*
1 yard purple	B2	Cut 4 strips 3" wide.
	Strip sets for striped diamond halves	Cut 11 strips 1½" wide.
⅔ yard aqua	A4, B4	Cut 7 strips 3" wide.
⅝ yard green	Strip sets for striped diamond halves	Cut 11 strips 1½" wide.
1¼ yards teal	Strip sets for striped diamond halves	Cut 11 strips 1½" wide.
	Double-fold binding	Cut 10 strips 2¼" wide.
4¾ yards black (If your fabric has 42" of usable width, make that 4⅛ yards.)	Background	Cut 7 strips 10½" wide. From each of 4 strips, cut 1 rectangle 10½" × 20½" and 1 square 10½" × 10½". Subcut the remaining strips into 8 more squares 10½" × 10½" for a total of 12 squares and 4 rectangles. (If you have 42" of usable fabric, you can cut the 12 squares and 4 rectangles from 5 strips 10½" wide.)
	Setting triangles	Cut 2 squares 15¾" × 15¾". Cut each twice diagonally to yield 8 triangles.
	Border 1 (narrow inner background border)	Cut 8 strips 2" wide. Piece 2 strips 2" × 69½" and 2 strips 2" × 72½".*
	Border 3 (wide outer border)	Cut 9 strips 6½" wide. Piece 2 strips 6½" × 74½" and 2 strips 6½" × 86½".*
2¾ yards 108"-wide fabric	Backing	
Batting: 94" × 94"		

Measure your finished quilt top and adjust the border lengths as needed. These measurements are for a quilt top that measures 69½" × 69½" before borders.

Block Assembly

DIAMOND BLOCK: TRIANGLE SIDE

1. Use the Striped Flying Geese triangle unit pattern (pattern pullout page P2) to make 32 freezer-paper templates of the unit. Or make 8 and use each 4 times.

2. Use the block maps as guides for color placement and to paper piece the triangle side of the diamond block. Make 16 of block A and 16 of block B.

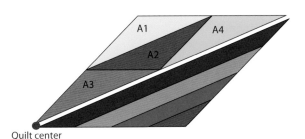

Quilt center

Striped Flying Geese diamond block A map
Make 16.

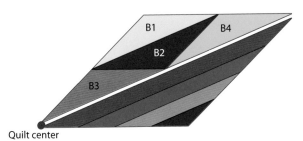

Quilt center

Striped Flying Geese diamond block B map
Make 16.

DIAMOND BLOCK: STRIP SETS

1. Stitch the 1½" strips into 11 strip sets, with the fabrics in the following order: fuchsia, teal, green, purple. Press the seam allowances toward the fuchsia.

2. Refer to the diagrams for Step 3 (next) and use the Striped Flying Geese triangle unit template pattern (pattern pullout page P2) as a guide to cut 16 strip-set triangles for both block A and block B. Every strip set will yield 3 triangles: 2 for one block and 1 for the other.

3. Cut 6 sets that yield 2 for block A and 1 for block B. Cut 5 sets that yield 1 for block A and 2 for block B. You'll have 1 extra piece for block A.

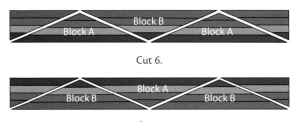

Cut 6.

Cut 5.
Cutting strip-set triangles

4. Sew the strip-set triangles from Step 3 to the paper-pieced triangles to complete the block. Follow the block maps to the left to make 16 of block A and 16 of block B.

Quilt Assembly

Follow the directions in General Piecing Instructions (page 5) to assemble the star and background and to add borders. Refer to the diagram for the Carpenter's Wheel setting (page 13).

Use the quilt assembly diagram as a guide for block placement.

Quilt assembly diagram

> **tip** To reduce the bulk in the center where 16 seams meet, stitch alternate blocks all the way to the center and trim excess seam allowances. To help align the points, leave the last few inches of the center open and hand baste before stitching.

JOSEPH'S COAT BLOCK

Desert Flower

74″ × 74″, by Cheryl Malkowski, 2009

Joseph's Coat square block

Joseph's Coat diamond block

◆ SKILL LEVEL: **Intermediate**

This is the first quilt I made for which I tried stretching blocks into diamonds, and I am still amazed at the result. If you'd like to make the single-star version, such as *Wine Harvest* by Rene Hyland (page 59) or *What Happened to My Box?* by Judy A. Byrd (also on page 59), refer to the fabric requirements and cutting instructions in the chart on page 29.

Fabric Requirements and Cutting Instructions

All requirements are based on 40" usable width of fabric. See General Piecing Instructions (page 5) for details on cutting methods as needed.

YARDAGE	FOR	CUTTING
¾ yard dark teal	A1	Cut 1 strip 3½" wide.
	B5, D5, E5, G5	Cut 4 strips 2½" wide.
	A5, H5	Cut 2 strips 4½" wide.
½ yard light aqua	A3	Cut 1 strip 3½" wide.
	B4, E4	Cut 3 strips 2" wide.
⅓ yard aqua	C2, F2	Cut 2 strips 2" wide.
	D1, G1	Cut 2 strips 2½" wide.
2⅝ yards cream	C4, F3	Cut 2 strips 2" wide.
	A4	Cut 1 strip 3½" wide.
	Outer Nine-Patch diamonds	Cut 5 strips 4" wide. Subcut into 30 diamonds, using the unit A template.*
	After cutting the above strips, remove the selvage from one edge of the remaining large piece and make a lengthwise cut 9" from that edge.	
	Outer Nine-Patch diamonds	From the 9"-wide piece, cut 2 lengthwise strips 4" wide × the length of the fabric. From these strips, cut 18 more diamonds, using the unit A template.*
	Setting squares	From the remaining 31"-wide piece, cut 8 squares 15¼" × 15¼".
2¾ yards brown	H2	Cut 1 strip 3½" wide.
	B2, E3	Cut 1 strip 2½" wide.
	C5, F5	Cut 4 strips 3" wide.
	Center piece and outer Nine-Patch diamonds	Cut 4 strips 4" wide. Subcut into 24 diamonds, using the unit A template.*
	Outer border	Cut 8 strips 2" wide. Piece 2 strips 2" × 71½" and 2 strips 2" × 74½".**
	Corner triangles	Cut 2 squares 22" × 22". Cut each square once diagonally to yield 4 triangles.
	Double-fold binding	Cut 9 strips 2¼" wide.
½ yard dark taupe	C1, D2, F1, G3	Cut 4 strips 2" wide.
	H1	Cut 1 strip 3½" wide.
⅝ yard dark aqua	D3, G2	Cut 1 strip 2½" wide.
	D4, G4	Cut 3 strips 2" wide
	Outer Nine-Patch diamonds	Cut 2 strips 4" wide. Subcut into 8 diamonds, using the unit A template.*
⅓ yard medium aqua	C3, F4	Cut 2 strips 2" wide.
½ yard green	B6, E7	Cut 2 strips 2" wide.
	B7, E6	Cut 2 strips 2½" wide.
	H3, H4	Cut 1 strip 3½" wide.
½ yard tan	D6, G7	Cut 2 strips 2½" wide.
	B3, D7, E2, G6	Cut 4 strips 2" wide.
⅓ yard aqua/cream print	A2	Cut 1 strip 3½" wide.
	B1, E1	Cut 2 strips 2½" wide.
2⅜ yards 108"-wide fabric	Backing	

Batting: 82" × 82"

*Or you can use the fast2cut Fussy Cutter 45° Diamond Guide rulers (see diagram, page 28, and Resources, page 64).
**Measure your finished quilt top and adjust the border lengths as needed. These measurements are for a quilt top that measures 71½" × 71½" before borders.

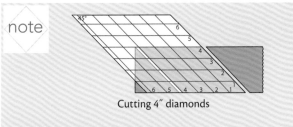

Cutting 4″ diamonds

Instead of using the unit A template to cut the outer Nine-Patch diamonds, you can use the fast2cut Fussy Cutter 45° Diamond Guide rulers (Resources, page 64).

Block Assembly

JOSEPH'S COAT BLOCK

1. Use the 4 Joseph's Coat unit patterns (pattern pullout page P6) to make 8 freezer-paper templates of each unit. Note that units A and H use the same pattern, as do units B and G, D and E, and C and F. Make 2 copies of each, 1 for each unit, and label each copy with the letters and numbers for that unit.

2. Use the block map as a guide for color placement and to stitch the units into rows. Press the seams in the A/B/C row toward unit C. Press the seams in the D/E row toward E. Press the seams in the F/G/H row toward H. Stitch the rows together and press toward the A/B/C row. Make 8 diamonds.

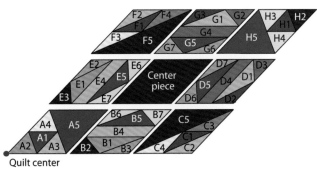

Joseph's Coat diamond block map
Make 8.

NINE-PATCH DIAMOND BLOCK

1. Use the diagram below to make 8 Nine-Patch diamond blocks.

2. Stitch the diamond-shaped units into rows and press toward the dark fabric.

3. Stitch the rows into diamond blocks and press the seam allowances to one side.

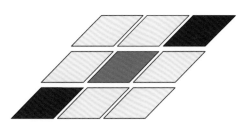

Nine-patch diamond block assembly
Make 8.

Quilt Assembly

Follow the directions in General Piecing Instructions (page 5) to assemble the star and background and to add border strips. Refer to the assembly diagram for the Rolling Star setting (page 13).

• QUILT VARIATION • Single-Star Version: Joseph's Coat

This version can be seen in Wine Harvest and What Happened to My Box? (page 59).

The following fabric requirements and cutting instructions are for a 67" × 67" quilt. All requirements are based on 40" usable width of fabric. See General Piecing Instructions (page 5) for details on cutting methods as needed.

YARDAGE	FOR	CUTTING
1¾ yards dark teal	A1	Cut 1 strip 3½" wide.
	B5, D5, E5, G5	Cut 4 strips 2½" wide.
	A5, H5	Cut 2 strips 4½" wide.
	Borders 2 and 4 (narrow contrasting borders)	Cut 13 strips 1½" wide. Piece 2 strips 1½" × 53½" and 2 strips 1½" × 55½" for border 2. Piece 2 strips 1½" × 65½" and 2 strips 1½" × 67½" for border 4.*
	Double-fold binding	Cut 8 strips 2¼" wide.
½ yard light aqua	A3	Cut 1 strip 3½" wide.
	B4, E4	Cut 3 strips 2" wide.
⅓ yard aqua	C2, F2	Cut 2 strips 2" wide.
	D1, G1	Cut 2 strips 2½" wide.
1⅞ yards cream	C4, F3	Cut 2 strips 2" wide.
	A4	Cut 1 strip 3½" wide.
	After cutting the above strips, remove the selvage from one edge of the remaining large piece and make a lengthwise cut 9" from that edge.	
	Border 1 (narrow background border)	From the 9"-wide piece, cut 2 strips 2" × 50½" and 2 strips 2" × 53½".*
	Setting squares and triangles	From the remaining 31"-wide piece, cut 4 squares 15¼" × 15¼" and 1 square 23" × 23". Cut the 23" square twice diagonally to yield 4 triangles.
⅞ yard brown	H2	Cut 1 strip 3½" wide.
	B2, E3	Cut 1 strip 2½" wide.
	C5, F5	Cut 4 strips 3" wide.
	Center piece	Cut 2 strips 4" wide. Subcut into 8 diamonds, using the unit A template.**
½ yard dark taupe	C1, D2, F1, G3	Cut 4 strips 2" wide.
	H1	Cut 1 strip 3½" wide.
⅜ yard dark aqua	D3, G2	Cut 1 strip 2½" wide.
	D4, G4	Cut 3 strips 2" wide.
⅓ yard medium aqua	C3, F4	Cut 2 strips 2" wide.
½ yard green	B6, E7	Cut 2 strips 2" wide.
	B7, E6	Cut 2 strips 2½" wide.
	H3, H4	Cut 1 strip 3½" wide.
½ yard tan	D6, G7	Cut 2 strips 2½" wide.
	B3, D7, E2, G6	Cut 4 strips 2" wide.
1½ yards aqua/cream print	A2	Cut 1 strip 3½" wide.
	B1, E1	Cut 2 strips 2½" wide.
	Border 3 (wide border)	Cut 7 strips 5½" wide. Piece 2 strips 5½" × 55½" and 2 strips 5½" × 65½".*
2¼ yards 108"-wide fabric	Backing	

Batting: 75" × 75"

*Measure your finished quilt top and adjust the border lengths as needed. These measurements are for a quilt top that measures 50½" × 50½" before borders. **Or you can use the fast2cut Fussy Cutter 45° Diamond Guide rulers (see illustration on page 28 and Resources on page 64).

NEW YORK BEAUTY BLOCK

Baja Sunrise

80″ × 80″, by Glenda Zalunardo, 2009

This simple design with sawtooth borders makes a spectacular quilt! For quilts made from the star only, see *Manhattan Star* (page 60) and *Blue Ice Swirl* by Sue Muckey (page 63). The fabric requirements and cutting instructions for the plain border version are given in the chart on page 33.

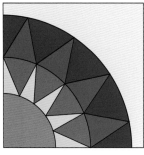

New York Beauty square block

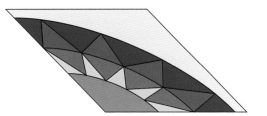

New York Beauty diamond block

Fabric Requirements and Cutting Instructions

All requirements are based on 40" usable width of fabric. See General Piecing Instructions (page 5) for details on cutting methods as needed.

YARDAGE	FOR	CUTTING
⅜ yard orange	A	Cut 8, using template pattern A on pattern pullout page P2.
1⅛ yards yellow	B1, B9	Cut 2 strips 2" wide.
	B3, B5, B7	Cut 2 strips 3" wide.
	Border 3 (second sawtooth border)	Cut 4 strips 4⅞" wide. Subcut into 32 squares 4⅞" × 4⅞".
		Cut 1 strip 4½" wide. Subcut into 4 squares 4½" × 4½".
½ yard green	B2, B4, B6, B8	Cut 4 strips 3½" wide.
4⅛ yards red	C1, C9	Cut 2 strips 3" wide.
	C3, C7	Cut 2 strips 4" wide.
	C5	Cut 1 strip 5" wide.
	Border 2 (first sawtooth border)	Cut 4 strips 4⅞" wide. Subcut into 28 squares 4⅞" × 4⅞".
	Border 4 (outer border)	Cut 8 strips 4½" wide. Piece 2 strips 4½" × 72½" and 2 strips 4½" × 80½".*
	Border 1 (narrow background top and bottom border)	Cut 3 strips 3½" wide. Piece 2 strips 3½" × 50½".*
	After cutting the above strips, remove the selvage from one edge of the remaining large piece and make a lengthwise cut 9" from that edge.	
	Border 1 (narrow background side borders)	From the 9"-wide piece, cut 2 strips 3½" × 56½" lengthwise along the selvage.*
	Setting squares and triangles	From the remaining 31"-wide piece, cut 4 squares 15¼" × 15¼" and 1 square 23" × 23". Cut the 23" square twice diagonally to yield 4 triangles.
1⅝ yards teal	C2, C8	Cut 2 strips 3" wide.
	C4, C6	Cut 2 strips 4" wide.
	Borders 2 and 3 (sawtooth borders)	Cut 8 strips 4⅞" wide. Subcut into 60 squares 4⅞" × 4⅞" and 4 squares 4½" × 4½".

Measure your finished quilt top and adjust the border lengths as needed. These measurements are for a quilt top that measures 50½" × 50½" before borders.

Continued on page 32

Continued from page 31

YARDAGE	FOR	CUTTING
1¼ yards cream/orange print	D	Cut 8, using template pattern D on pattern pullout page P3.
⅝ yard related fabric	Double-fold binding	Cut 9 strips 2¼" wide.
2½ yards 108"-wide fabric	Backing	
Batting: 88" × 88"		

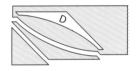

Cutting unit D

Block Assembly

1. Use the 4 New York Beauty unit patterns (pattern pullout pages P2–P4) to make the freezer-paper templates. Make 1 freezer-paper template each of units A and D and 8 each of units B and C. The templates for the A and D units can be reused 8 times.

2. Use the registration marks (dots) on units A and D to mark the fabric. The dots mark the intersections of the points on the neighboring units.

3. Use the block map as a guide for color placement.

4. Stitch the units together in order: A to D. Press the seam allowances toward D. Make 8 diamonds.

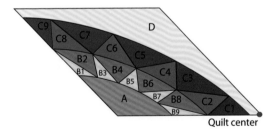

Quilt center

New York Beauty diamond block map
Make 8.

Quilt Assembly

Follow the directions in General Piecing Instructions (page 5) to assemble the star and background and to add the border strips for border 1.

1. To make border 2, use your favorite method to make 56 half-square triangle 4½" × 4½" unfinished blocks from the teal and red 4⅞" squares. Press toward the teal. Stitch together in 4 sets of 14 sawteeth each. Add 4½" teal squares to both ends of 2 of the sets. Use the project photo (page 30) and quilt assembly diagram as guides.

2. To make border 3, use the teal and yellow 4⅞" squares to make 64 half-square triangle 4½" × 4½" blocks. Press toward the teal. Stitch together in 4 sets of 16 sawteeth each. Add 4½" yellow squares to both ends of 2 of the sets. Use the project photo (page 30) and quilt assembly diagram as guides.

3. Add the short pieced borders to the top and bottom of the quilt and the long pieced borders to the sides of the quilt. Press all the seams to the outside. Add the border strips for border 4.

Quilt assembly diagram

• QUILT VARIATION •

Single-Star Version: New York Beauty

This version can be seen in Manhattan Star *(page 60) and*
Blue Ice Swirl *(page 63).*

The following fabric requirements and cutting instructions are for a 53" × 53"
quilt. All requirements are based on 40" usable width of fabric. See General
Piecing Instructions (page 5) for details on cutting methods as needed.

YARDAGE	FOR	CUTTING
⅜ yard orange	A	Cut 8, using template pattern A on pattern pullout page P2.
⅜ yard yellow	B1, B9	Cut 2 strips 2" wide.
	B3, B5, B7	Cut 2 strips 3" wide.
½ yard green	B2, B4, B6, B8	Cut 4 strips 3½" wide.
2⅝ yards red	C1, C9	Cut 2 strips 3" wide.
	C3, C7	Cut 2 strips 4" wide.
	C5	Cut 1 strip 5" wide.
	Double-fold binding	Cut 6 strips 2¼" wide.
	After cutting the above strips, remove the selvage from one edge of the remaining large strip and make a lengthwise cut 9" from that edge.	
	Narrow background border	From the 9"-wide piece, cut 2 strips 2" × 50½" and 2 strips 2" × 53½".*
	Setting squares and triangles	From the remaining 31"-wide piece, cut 4 squares 15¼" × 15¼" and 1 square 23" × 23". Cut the 23" square twice diagonally to yield 4 triangles.
½ yard teal	C2, C8	Cut 2 strips 3" wide.
	C4, C6	Cut 2 strips 4" wide.
1¼ yards cream/orange print	D	Cut 8, using template pattern D on pattern pullout page P3.
1¾ yards 108"-wide fabric	Backing	

Batting: 61" × 61"

*Measure your finished quilt top and adjust the border lengths as needed. These measure-
ments are for a quilt top that measures 50½" × 50½" before borders.

OPTICAL ILLUSION BLOCK

Wintermint

65″ × 65″, by Cheryl Malkowski, 2009

◆ **SKILL LEVEL: Confident Beginner**

Some slight revisions were made to this traditional block to make it simpler to piece and to add drama to the diamond.

Optical Illusion square block   Optical Illusion diamond block

Fabric Requirements
and Cutting Instructions

All requirements are based on 40" usable width of fabric. See General Piecing Instructions (page 5) for details on cutting methods as needed.

YARDAGE	FOR	CUTTING
1 yard purple	A2, B2, C4, D3, E2	Cut 7 strips 3" wide.
	E4	Cut 2 strips 2½" wide.
	E8	Cut 1 strip 5½" wide.
⅞ yard fuchsia	A1, B4, B6, C2	Cut 4 strips 3" wide.
	E7	Cut 1 strip 5½" wide.
	Border 2 (narrow contrasting border)	Cut 6 strips 1½" wide. Piece 2 strips 1½" × 53½" and 2 strips 1½" × 55½".*
½ yard pink	B5, C1, D1, E6	Cut 4 strips 3" wide.
2 yards dark green	B3, C3, D4	Cut 4 strips 3" wide.
	After cutting the above strips, remove the selvage from one edge of the remaining large piece and make a lengthwise cut 9" from that edge.	
	Border 1 (narrow background border)	From the 9"-wide piece, cut 2 strips 2" × 50½" and 2 pieces 2" × 53½".*
	Setting squares and triangles	From the remaining 31"-wide piece, cut 4 squares 15¼" × 15¼" and 1 square 23" × 23". Cut the 23" square twice diagonally to yield 4 triangles.
⅞ yard light green	B1, B7, D2, E1, E5	Cut 6 strips 3" wide.
	C5, E3	Cut 3 strips 2½" wide.
1¾ yards purple print	Border 3 (outer border)	Cut 7 strips 5½" wide. Piece 2 strips 5½" × 55½" and 2 strips 5½" × 65½".*
	Double-fold binding	Cut 8 strips 2¼" wide.
2⅛ yards 108"-wide fabric	Backing	
Batting: 73" × 73"		

*Measure your finished quilt top and adjust the border lengths as needed. These measurements are for a quilt top that measures 50½" × 50½" before borders.

Block Assembly

1. Use the 5 Optical Illusion unit patterns (pattern pullout pages P1 and P2) to make 8 freezer-paper templates of each unit.

2. Use the block map as a guide for color placement and to stitch the units into a diamond. Stitch A to B and press toward unit A.

3. Stitch A/B to the remaining units and press toward unit E. Make 8 diamonds.

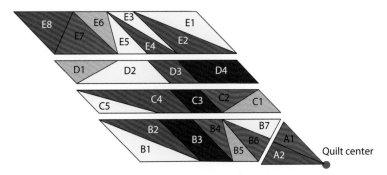

Optical Illusion diamond block map
Make 8.

Quilt Assembly

Follow the directions in General Piecing Instructions (page 5) to assemble the star and background and to add border strips.

ROLLING SQUARES BLOCK

Radiant Jewels

53″ × 53″, by Nancy Jarvis, quilted by Denise Shelton, 2009

◆ SKILL LEVEL: **Confident Beginner**

I love the lacy look of this star. You can put it into a Rolling Star setting by making 16 diamonds instead of 8 and by cutting 8 of the large squares and 4 triangles for the corners. Check out *Rubies Star* by Ruby Kosola (page 57) for an example made by a quilter who did just that.

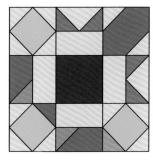

Rolling Squares square block

Rolling Squares diamond block

Fabric Requirements and Cutting Instructions

All requirements are based on 40" usable width of fabric. See General Piecing
Instructions (page 5) for details on cutting methods as needed.

YARDAGE	FOR	CUTTING
3½ yards lavender	A2, A3, C3, C4, F3, F4, H3, H4	Cut 8 strips 2" wide.
	B1, B4, D1, D4, D6, G3	Cut 8 strips 3" wide.
	C2, C5, F2, F5, H5	Cut 3 strips 3½" wide.
	Double-fold binding	Cut 6 strips 2¼" wide.
	After cutting the above strips, remove the selvage from one edge of the remaining large piece and make a lengthwise cut 9" from that edge.	
	Narrow background border	From the 9"-wide piece, cut 2 strips 2" × 50½" and 2 strips 2" × 53½".*
	Setting squares and triangles	From the remaining 31"-wide piece, cut 4 squares 15¼" × 15¼" and 1 square 23" × 23". Cut the 23" square twice diagonally to yield 4 triangles.
½ yard aqua mottle	C1, F1, H1	Cut 4 strips 3" wide.
⅝ yard fuchsia	A1, E1, G1	Cut 5 strips 3" wide.
	H2	Cut 1 strip 3½" wide.
⅜ yard dark blue	D5	Cut 2 strips 4½" wide.
¼ yard blue	E2, G2	Cut 2 strips 2" wide.
⅓ yard sage	B2, D2	Cut 2 strips 2" wide.
	B3, D3	Cut 1 strip 3½" wide.
1¾ yards 108"-wide fabric	Backing	

Batting: 61" × 61"

*Measure your finished quilt top and adjust the border lengths as needed. These measurements
are for a quilt top that measures 50½" × 50½" before borders.

Block Assembly

1. Use the 6 Rolling Squares unit patterns (pattern pullout pages P3–P5) to make 8 freezer-paper templates of each unit. Note that units C, F, and H use the same pattern. Make 3 copies of that pattern, 1 for each unit, and label each with the letters and numbers for that unit.

2. Use the block map as a guide for color placement and to stitch the units into rows. Press the seams in the A/B/C row toward unit A. Press the seams in the D/E row toward E. Press the seams in the F/G/H row toward F.

3. Stitch the rows together and press toward the F/G/H row. Make 8 diamonds.

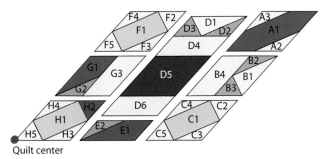

Quilt center

Rolling Squares diamond block map
Make 8.

Quilt Assembly

Follow the directions in General Piecing Instructions (page 5) to assemble the star and background and to add border strips.

Tropical Vista

89″ × 89″, by Glenda Zalunardo, 2009

◆ **SKILL LEVEL: Intermediate**

If you prefer to make a single star, such as *Ocean Starburst* by Sharon Hager (page 61), the fabric requirements and cutting instructions are given in the chart on page 42.

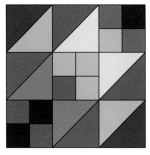

Steps to the Altar square block

Steps to the Altar diamond block

Fabric Requirements and Cutting Instructions

All requirements are based on 40" usable width of fabric. See General Piecing Instructions (page 5) for details on cutting methods as needed.

YARDAGE	FOR	CUTTING
1 yard green	B4, C4, E2, F2	Cut 11 strips 3" wide.
1 yard dark blue	A2, B2, B6, F6	Cut 11 strips 3" wide.
4¼ yards midnight blue	Corner triangles	Cut 2 squares 22" × 22". Cut each square once diagonally to yield 4 triangles.
	A1, E1, F1	From the width remaining from the 22" squares, cut 6 lengthwise strips 3" × 44".
	Border 1 (narrow background border)	Cut 8 strips 3" wide. Piece 2 strips 3" × 71½" and 2 strips 3" × 76½".*
	Border 3 (outer border)	Cut 9 strips 6" wide. Piece 2 strips 6" × 78½" and 2 strips 6" × 89½".*
	Double-fold binding	Cut 10 strips 2¼" wide.
⅔ yard dark teal	D3, F3	Cut 7 strips 3" wide.
⅔ yard sage	B3, C3	Cut 7 strips 3" wide.
⅞ yard medium blue	D1, D4, F4	Cut 9 strips 3" wide.
2¾ yards spring green	B5, C2, D2, F5	Cut 11 strips 3" wide.
	Setting squares	Cut 8 squares 15¼" × 15¼".
⅞ yard aqua	B1, C1	Cut 5 strips 3" wide.
	Border 2 (narrow contrasting border)	Cut 8 strips 1½" wide. Piece 2 strips 1½" × 76½" and 2 strips 1½" × 78½".*
2¾ yards 108"-wide fabric	Backing	

Batting: 97" × 97"

Measure your finished quilt top and adjust the border lengths as needed. These measurements are for a quilt top that measures 71½" × 71½" before borders.

Block Assembly

1. Use the 3 Steps to the Altar unit patterns (pattern pullout pages P3 and P5) to make 8 freezer-paper templates of each unit. Note that units A and E use the same pattern, as do B and F, and C and D. Make 2 copies each of those patterns, 1 for each unit, and label each copy with the numbers and letters for that unit. Either reuse the freezer-paper templates to make 16 blocks or copy double the number of patterns.

2. Use the block map as a guide for color placement and to stitch the units into rows. Stitch A to B and press toward A. Stitch C to D and press toward C. Stitch E to F and press toward F.

3. Stitch the rows together and press toward the A/B row. You will need to do some creative nesting with the middle row because of the piecing order. Make 16 diamonds.

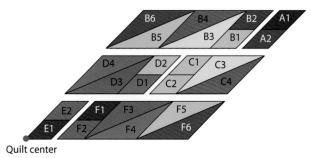

Quilt center

Steps to the Altar diamond block map
Make 16.

Quilt Assembly

Follow the directions in General Piecing Instructions (page 5) to assemble the star and background and to add border strips. Refer to the assembly diagram for the Rolling Star setting (page 13).

• QUILT VARIATION •

Single-Star Version: Steps to the Altar

This version can be seen in Ocean Starburst *(page 61).*

The following fabric requirements and cutting instructions are for a 53" × 53" quilt. All requirements are based on 40" usable width of fabric. See General Piecing Instructions (page 5) for details on cutting methods as needed.

YARDAGE	FOR	CUTTING
1 yard green	B4, C4, E2, F2	Cut 6 strips 3" wide.
	Binding	Cut 6 strips 2¼" wide.
⅝ yard dark blue	A2, B2, B6, F6	Cut 6 strips 3" wide.
⅓ yard midnight blue	A1, E1, F1	Cut 3 strips 3" wide.
½ yard dark teal	D3, F3	Cut 4 strips 3" wide.
½ yard sage	B3, C3	Cut 4 strips 3" wide.
1⅝ yards light gold	Remove the selvage from one edge of fabric and make a lengthwise cut 9" from that edge.	
	Narrow background border	From the 9"-wide piece, cut 2 strips 2" × 50½" and 2 strips 2" × 53½".*
	Setting squares and triangles	From the remaining 31"-wide piece, cut 4 squares 15¼" × 15¼" and 1 square 23" × 23". Cut the 23" square twice diagonally to yield 4 triangles.
½ yard medium blue	D1, D4, F4	Cut 5 strips 3" wide.
⅝ yard spring green	B5, C2, D2, F5	Cut 6 strips 3" wide.
¼ yard aqua	B1, C1	Cut 2 strips 3" wide.
1¾ yards 108"-wide fabric	Backing	
Batting: 61" × 61"		

*Measure your finished quilt top and adjust the border lengths as needed. These measurements are for a quilt top that measures 50½" × 50½" before borders.

STORM AT SEA BLOCK

Tuscan Star

65″ × 65″, by Donna DeFea, quilted by Jane Yurk, 2009

◆ **SKILL LEVEL: Confident Beginner**

This block makes a beautiful star with either end of the diamond in the center. To see examples of this, check out *Prairie Storm* by Cheryl Meredith (page 57), *Golden Diamonds* by Leila Dixon (page 61), and *Pumpkin Spice* (page 62). Experiment after you finish the blocks to see which you like better!

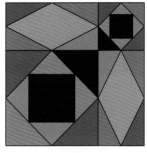

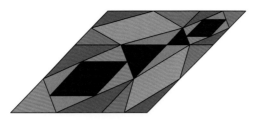

Storm at Sea square block   Storm at Sea diamond block

Fabric Requirements
and Cutting Instructions

All requirements are based on 40" usable width of fabric. See General Piecing
Instructions (page 5) for details on cutting methods as needed.

YARDAGE	FOR	CUTTING
½ yard light green	A4, A5	Cut 1 strip 2" wide.
	C2, C3	Cut 2 strips 3" wide.
	C9	Cut 1 strip 4½" wide.
1⅝ yards pale gold	Remove the selvage from one edge of the fabric and make a lengthwise cut 9" from that edge.	
	Border 1 (narrow background border)	From the 9"-wide piece, cut 2 strips 2" × 50½" and 2 strips 2" × 53½".*
	Setting squares and triangles	From the remaining 31"-wide piece, cut 4 squares 15¼" × 15¼" and 1 square 23" × 23". Cut the 23" square twice diagonally to yield 4 triangles.
⅝ yard gold	A2, A3	Cut 1 strip 2" wide.
	B3, D3	Cut 3 strips 2½" wide.
	C4, C5	Cut 2 strips 3" wide.
⅞ yard green	A6, A7	Cut 2 strips 2" wide.
	B4, D4	Cut 3 strips 2½" wide.
	C6, C7	Cut 4 strips 3" wide.
⅝ yard aqua	A8, B2, B5, D2, D5	Cut 6 strips 3" wide.
1 yard purple	C1, C8	Cut 3 strips 4½" wide.
	A1, A9	Cut 2 strips 3" wide.
	Border 2 (narrow contrasting border)	Cut 6 strips 1½" wide. Piece 2 strips 1½" × 53½" and 2 strips 1½" × 55½".*
½ yard tan/lavender print	B1, D1	Cut 4 strips 3½" wide.
1¼ yards gold/multicolored print	Border 3 (outer border)	Cut 7 strips 5½" wide. Piece 2 strips 5½" × 55½" and 2 strips 5½" × 65½".*
⅝ yard related fabric	Binding	Cut 8 strips 2¼" wide.
2⅛ yards 108"-wide fabric	Backing	
Batting: 73" × 73"		

*Measure your finished quilt top and adjust the border lengths as needed. These measurements
are for a quilt top that measures 50½" × 50½" before borders.

Block Assembly

1. Use the 4 Storm at Sea unit patterns (pattern pullout pages P2–P4) to make 8 freezer-paper templates of each unit.

2. Use the block map as a guide for color placement and to stitch the units into rows. Stitch A to B and press toward B. Stitch C to D and press toward D.

3. Stitch the rows together and press toward the A/B row. Make 8 diamonds.

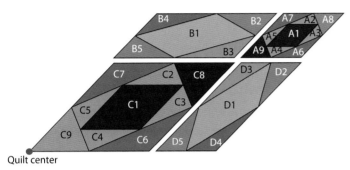

Quilt center

Storm at Sea diamond block map
Make 8.

Quilt Assembly

Follow the directions in General Piecing instructions (page 5) to assemble the star and background and to add border strips.

SUMMER WINDS BLOCK

Frost on the Window

90″ × 90″, by Cheryl Malkowski, 2009

◆ SKILL LEVEL: **Skilled Beginner**

This quilt incorporates diamond and square blocks, and even some triangle blocks that are half of the squares. If you prefer to make a star only, such as *Sunburst* by Sarah Huie (page 62), the fabric requirements and cutting instructions are provided in the chart on page 51.

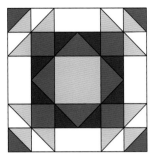

Summer Winds square block   Summer Winds diamond block

Fabric Requirements and Cutting Instructions

All requirements are based on 40" usable width of fabric. See General Piecing Instructions (page 5) for details on cutting methods as needed.

YARDAGE	FOR	CUTTING
6 yards navy	B6, B9, C7, D1	Cut 4 strips 2" wide.
	A1, A3, E7, E9	Cut 4 strips 2½" wide.
	A5, C3, C8, D5, D8, E3	Cut 6 strips 3" wide.
	Border 2 (pieced border)	Cut 1 strip 3⅜" wide. Subcut into 6 squares 3⅜" × 3⅜". Cut each twice diagonally to yield 24 triangles.
		Cut 2 strips 3" wide. Subcut into 24 squares 3" × 3". Cut each once diagonally to yield 48 triangles.
		Cut 3 strips 2⅝" wide. Subcut into 24 rectangles 2⅝" × 4¾".
		Cut 2 strips 2⅜" wide. Subcut into 24 squares 2⅜" × 2⅜". Cut each once diagonally to yield 48 triangles.
		Cut 1 strip 2" wide. Subcut into 8 rectangles 2" × 3½".
		Cut 1 strip 9⅞" wide. Subcut into 4 squares 9⅞" × 9⅞". Cut each once diagonally to yield 8 triangles.
		Cut 2 squares 19¼" × 19¼". Cut each twice diagonally to yield 8 triangles.
	Border 1 (narrow background border)	Cut 2 strips 2½" wide. Piece 1 strip 2½" × 50½".*
	Border 5 (narrow outer border)	Cut 9 strips 2" wide. Piece 2 strips 2" × 87½" and 2 strips 2" × 90½".*
	Double-fold binding	Cut 10 strips 2¼" wide.
	After cutting the above strips, remove the selvage from one edge of the remaining large piece and make a lengthwise cut 9" from that edge.	
	Border 1 (narrow background border)	From the 9"-wide piece, cut 1 strip 2½" × 50½" and 2 strips 2½" × 54½".*
	Setting squares and triangles	From the remaining 31"-wide piece, cut 4 squares 15¼" × 15¼" and 1 square 23" × 23". Cut the 23" square twice diagonally to yield 4 triangles.

Measure your finished quilt top and adjust the border lengths as needed. These measurements are for a quilt top that measures 50½" × 50½" before borders.

Continued on page 48

Continued from page 47

YARDAGE	FOR	CUTTING
3½ yards light blue	B8, D2	Cut 2 strips 2″ wide.
	A2, A4, E6, E8	Cut 4 strips 2½″ wide.
	A6, A8, B2, E2	Cut 3 strips 3″ wide
	C1	Cut 2 strips 4½″ wide.
	Border 2 (pieced border)	Cut 1 strip 3⅜″ wide. Subcut into 6 squares 3⅜″ × 3⅜″. Cut each twice diagonally to yield 24 triangles. Cut 3 strips 3″ wide. Subcut into 30 squares 3″ × 3″. Cut each once diagonally to yield 60 triangles. Cut 1 strip 5⅛″ wide. Subcut into 6 squares 5⅛″ × 5⅛″. Cut each once diagonally to yield 12 triangles.
		Cut 1 strip 3½″ wide. Subcut into 4 squares 3½″ × 3½″.
		Cut 2 strips 2⅜″ wide. Subcut into 20 squares 2⅜″ × 2⅜″. Cut each once diagonally to yield 40 triangles.
	Border 4 (wide contrasting border)	Cut 9 strips 6½″ wide. Piece 2 strips 6½″ × 75½″ and 2 strips 6½″ × 87½″.*
1⅛ yards medium blue	B3, B7, D3, D6	Cut 4 strips 3″ wide.
	Border 3 (narrow contrasting border)	Cut 8 strips 2″ wide. Piece 2 strips 2″ × 72½″ and 2 strips 2″ × 75½″.*
	Border 2 (pieced border)	Cut 1 strip 3″ wide. Subcut into 12 squares 3″ × 3″. Cut each once diagonally to yield 24 triangles. Cut 1 strip 2⅝″ wide. Subcut into 12 squares 2⅝″ × 2⅝″. Cut 1 strip 2″ wide. Subcut into 16 squares 2″ × 2″.
1⅛ yards royal blue	A9, B5, C2, C5, D4, D7, E4	Cut 6 strips 3″ wide.
	Border 2 (pieced border)	Cut 1 strip 3″ wide. Subcut into 6 squares 3″ × 3″. Cut each once diagonally to yield 12 triangles. Cut 1 strip 5½″ wide. Subcut into 6 squares 5½″ × 5½″. Cut each twice diagonally to yield 24 triangles. Cut 1 strip 4¼″ wide. Subcut into 2 squares 4¼″ × 4¼″. Cut each twice diagonally to yield 8 triangles. From the remnant of the 4¼″-wide strip, subcut 6 squares 2⅜″ × 2⅜″. Cut each once diagonally to yield 12 triangles. Cut 1 strip 2″ wide. Subcut into 8 rectangles 2″ × 3⅞″.
⅞ yard white print	A7, B1, B4, C4, C6, E1, E5	Cut 6 strips 3″ wide.
	Border 2 (pieced border)	Cut 2 strips 3″ wide. Subcut into 24 squares 3″ × 3″. Cut each once diagonally to yield 48 triangles.
	Border 2 (pieced border)	Cut 1 strip 2⅜″ wide. Subcut into 10 squares 2⅜″ × 2⅜″. Cut each once diagonally to yield 20 triangles. Cut 1 strip 2″ wide. Subcut into 8 rectangles 2″ × 3½″.
2¾ yards 108″-wide fabric	Backing	
Batting: 98″ × 98″		

**Measure your finished quilt top and adjust the border lengths as needed. These measurements are for a quilt top that measures 50½″ × 50½″ before borders.*

Diamond Block Assembly

1. Use the 4 Summer Winds unit patterns (pattern pullout page P1) to make 8 freezer-paper templates of each unit. Note that units A and E use the same pattern; so make 2 copies of that unit and label each copy with the letters and numbers for that unit. Also notice that the numbering starts at opposite ends for A and E.

2. Use the block map as a guide for color placement and to stitch the units into rows. You will need to do some creative nesting between the C unit and the B and D units on either side because of the order in which unit C needs to be pieced.

3. Stitch the rows together and press toward row E. Make 8 diamonds.

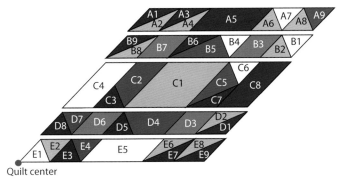

Quilt center

Summer Winds diamond block map
Make 8.

Triangle Border Assembly

TRIANGLE BORDER BLOCKS

1. Using the half-square triangles cut from the 3″ light blue, royal blue, navy, and white squares, piece the following half-square triangle squares. Arrows indicate the pressing direction.

Make 12 light
blue / royal blue.

Make 12 light
blue / white.

Make 12 light
blue / white.

Make 24
navy / light blue.

2. Using the quarter-square triangles cut from the royal blue 5½″ squares and the half-square triangles cut from the white and navy 3″ squares, piece the following Flying Geese. Arrows indicate the pressing direction.

Make 12 navy /
royal blue / white.

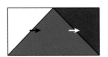

Make 12 white /
royal blue / navy.

3. Using the quarter-square triangles cut from the navy and light blue 3⅜″ squares, piece the following triangles. Press toward the navy.

Make 12 navy / light blue.

Make 12 light blue / navy.

4. Refer to the triangle block assembly diagram to piece 12 triangle border blocks together. Press the seam allowances in each row in the same direction and alternate directions between rows.

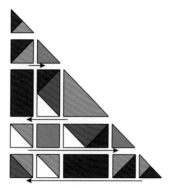

Triangle block assembly

CORNER SQUARE BLOCKS

1. Using the half-square triangles cut from the royal blue, light blue, white, and navy 2⅜" squares, make the following half-square triangle squares. Arrows indicate the pressing direction.

Make 4 light blue / royal blue.   Make 4 light blue / white.   Make 8 light blue / white.

Make 12 navy / light blue.   Make 12 navy / light blue.   Make 4 navy / royal blue.   Make 4 navy / royal blue.

2. Using the quarter-square triangles cut from the royal blue 4¼" squares and the half-square triangles cut from the white and navy 2⅜" squares, piece the following Flying Geese. Arrows indicate the pressing direction.

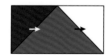 

Make 4 navy / royal blue / white.   Make 4 white / royal blue / navy.

3. Stack pairs of the royal blue 2" × 3⅞" rectangles right sides together. Cut a 45° angle from one end of each set.

4. Using the strips cut in Step 3 and the half-square triangles cut from the navy 2⅜" squares, make the following chisel units. Arrows indicate the pressing direction.

Make 4 navy / royal blue.

Make 4 royal blue / navy.

5. Refer to the corner square block assembly diagram to piece 4 corner blocks. Press the seam allowances in each row in the same direction and alternate directions between rows.

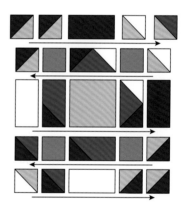

Corner square block assembly
Make 4.

TRIANGLE BORDER STRIPS

Refer to the triangle border assembly diagram to assemble 4 triangle border strips. Use the triangle border blocks, the half-square triangles cut from the 9⅞" squares, and quarter-square triangles cut from the 19¼" squares. Press the seam allowances to one side.

Triangle border assembly
Make 4.

Quilt Assembly

Follow the directions in General Piecing Instructions (page 5) to assemble the star and background and to add border 1 strips.

1. To add border 2, stitch a triangle border unit to each side of the quilt center. Press toward the center.

2. Stitch a square corner block to each end of the 2 remaining triangle border units. Stitch to the top and bottom of the quilt and press toward the center.

• QUILT VARIATION •

Single-Star Version: Summer Winds

This version can be seen in Sunburst (page 62).

The following fabric requirements and cutting instructions are for a 54" × 54" quilt. All requirements are based on 40" usable width of fabric. See General Piecing Instructions (page 5) for details on cutting methods as needed.

YARDAGE	FOR	CUTTING
3⅛ yards navy	B6, B9, C7, D1	Cut 4 strips 2" wide.
	A1, A3, E7, E9	Cut 4 strips 2½" wide.
	A5, C3, C8, D5, D8, E3	Cut 6 strips 3" wide.
	Double-fold binding	Cut 6 strips 2¼" wide.
	Narrow background border	Cut 2 strips 2½" wide. Piece 1 strip 2½" × 50½".*
	After cutting the above strips, remove the selvage from one edge of the remaining large piece and make a lengthwise cut 9" from that edge.	
	Narrow background border	From the 9"-wide piece, cut 1 strip 2½" × 50½" and 2 strips 2½" × 54½".*
	Setting squares and triangles	From the remaining 31"-wide piece, cut 4 squares 15¼" × 15¼" and 1 square 23" × 23". Cut the 23" square twice diagonally to yield 4 triangles.
⅔ yard light blue	B8, D2	Cut 2 strips 2" wide.
	A2, A4, E6, E8	Cut 4 strips 2½" wide.
	A6, A8, B2, E2	Cut 3 strips 3" wide.
⅜ yard medium blue	B3, B7, D3, D6	Cut 4 strips 3" wide.
⅝ yard royal blue	A9, B5, C2, C5, D4, D7, E4	Cut 6 strips 3" wide.
⅝ yard white print	A7, B1, B4, C4, C6, E1, E5	Cut 6 strips 3" wide.
1¾ yards 108"-wide fabric	Backing	

Batting: 62" × 62"

Measure your finished quilt top and adjust the border lengths as needed. These instructions are for a quilt top that measures 50½" × 50½" before borders.

WOVEN LOGS BLOCK

Solar Flare

90″ × 90″, by Ramonda Weckerle, 2009

◆ SKILL LEVEL: **Skilled Beginner**

This intricate-looking design is actually so simple it doesn't require any paper piecing at all! Mostly strip pieced, it goes together very quickly. A single-star version is also included in the chart on page 56. *Callie Lily* by Lora Bateson (page 62) is an example of this. Time to play with gradating colors!

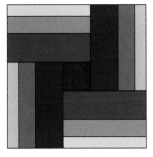

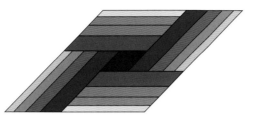

Woven Logs square block | Woven Logs diamond block

Fabric Requirements and Cutting Instructions

All requirements are based on 40" usable width of fabric. See General Piecing Instructions (page 5) for details on cutting methods as needed.

YARDAGE	FOR	CUTTING
Yellow to red (YR1–YR4)		
⅝ yard YR1	Block X, block Y, border 2 (pieced border)	Cut 11 strips 1⅛" wide.
	Square block Z	Cut 4 strips 1⅜" wide.
¾ yard YR2	Block X, block Y, border 2 (pieced border)	Cut 11 strips 1⅜" wide.
	Square block Z	Cut 4 strips 1¾" wide.
⅞ yard YR3	Block X, block Y, border 2 (pieced border)	Cut 11 strips 1⅝" wide.
	Square block Z	Cut 4 strips 2⅛" wide.
1 yard YR4	Block X, block Y, border 2 (pieced border)	Cut 10 strips 2⅛" wide.
	Square block Z	Cut 4 strips 2¾" wide.
Lavender to purple (P1–P4)		
⅝ yard P1	Block X, block Y, border 2 (pieced border)	Cut 11 strips 1⅛" wide.
	Square block Z	Cut 4 strips 1⅜" wide.
¾ yard P2	Block X, block Y, border 2 (pieced border)	Cut 11 strips 1⅜" wide.
	Square block Z	Cut 4 strips 1¾" wide.
⅞ yard P3	Block X, block Y, border 2 (pieced border)	Cut 11 strips 1⅝" wide.
	Square block Z	Cut 4 strips 2⅛" wide.
1 yard P4	Block X, block Y, border 2 (pieced border)	Cut 9 strips 2⅛" wide.
	Square block Z	Cut 4 strips 2¾" wide.

Continued on page 54

Continued from page 53

YARDAGE	FOR	CUTTING
Yellow to red (YR1–YR4)		
3⅝ yards black	Diamond centers of blocks X, Y	Cut 2 strips 2½" wide. Cut one end of each strip with the ruler at a 45° angle. Subcut into 16 diamonds by measuring 2½" from that angled cut.*
	Square centers of block Z	Cut 1 strip 3¼" wide. Subcut into 8 squares 3¼" × 3¼".
	Setting corner triangles	Cut 2 squares 21¾" × 21¾". Cut each once diagonally to yield 4 triangles.
	Border 1 (narrow background border)	Cut 8 strips 3" wide. Piece 2 strips 3" × 71½" and 2 strips 3" × 76½".**
	Border 3 (outer border)	Cut 9 strips 5½" wide. Piece 2 strips 5½" × 80½" and 2 strips 5½" × 90½".**
¾ yard related fabric	Double-fold binding	Cut 10 strips 2¼" wide.
2¾ yards 108"-wide fabric	Backing	
Batting: 98" × 98"		

*Or you can use the fast2cut Fussy Cutter 45° Diamond Guide rulers (see diagram on page 28 and Resources on page 64).
**Measure your finished quilt top and adjust the border lengths as needed. These measurements are for a quilt top that measures 71½" × 71½" before borders.

Strip Sets

1. Make 8 strip sets from 8 strips each of YR1–YR4 fabrics labeled for blocks X and Y. Stagger 4 strip sets to the left and 4 to the right at approximately 45°, as in the illustrations below. Note that the narrowest strips are the lightest color. As the strips get wider, the color gets darker. Press toward the darkest fabric.

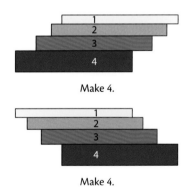

Make 4.

Make 4.

2. Repeat with 8 purple strips P1–P4. Press toward the darkest fabric.

3. Place a YR1–YR4 strip set on your cutting board, with the lightest color farthest away from you. Make a 45°-angle cut from the left side of the strip set to clean off the selvage edges.

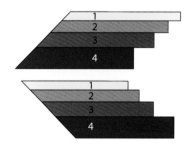

45°-angle cut from left side of each strip set

4. Place the 6⅝" line of a wide ruler along the new diagonal edge and cut. Cut 4 from each strip set according to the way the strip is slanted, for a total of 32.

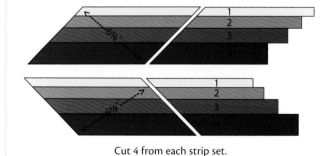

Cut 4 from each strip set.

5. Repeat Steps 3 and 4 for the P1–P4 (purple) strip sets.

6. Make 4 strip sets from the 4 strips each of the YR1–YR4 fabrics labeled for the square block Z, but do not stagger them at a 45° angle. The colors are arranged the same as for blocks X and Y, but press the seam allowances toward the lightest fabric. Cut 16 strips 9¼" long from the 4 strip sets. Repeat with the purple strip sets.

Block Assembly

Block X for outside ring
Make 8.

Block Y for center star
Make 8.

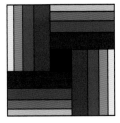

Block Z for setting squares
Make 8.

1. To start sewing each unit, stitch the long end of fabric 4 (on a YR strip set) to the black center, stopping about 1" from the end of the seam.

Stitch partial seam.

2. Continue to stitch the striped units clockwise around the center, matching the outside edges, until all the seams are finished except the first.

3. Go back and finish up the first seam.

Quilt Assembly

Follow the directions in General Piecing Instructions (page 5) to assemble the star and background and to add border strips. Refer to the instructions for the Rolling Star setting (page 13), keeping in mind that you will place pieced blocks in places that may be referred to as background in the general instructions.

Refer to the quilt assembly diagram and the project photo (page 52) to set the blocks in place on a design wall or surface.

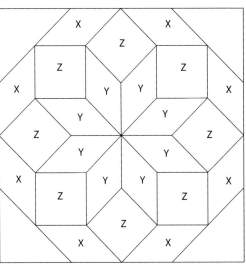

Woven Logs quilt assembly diagram

Pieced Border Assembly

1. Make the following strip sets for the pieced border:

   2 of YR1–YR4

   1 of YR1–YR3

   1 of P1–P4

   2 of P1–P3

2. Cut the strip sets into 2½" pieces. You need the following:

   32 pieces from the YR1–YR4 sets; remove YR4 from 4 of the units and add them to the YR1–YR3 pile

   16 pieces from the YR1–YR3 set (20, including the 4 created from the YR1–YR4 sets)

   16 pieces from the P1–P4 set

   24 pieces from the P1–P3 sets

3. Cut 4 squares 2½" × 2½" from remnants of P3 fabric for the border corners.

4. To piece border 2, stitch the pieced border pieces together using the illustrations below as a guide.

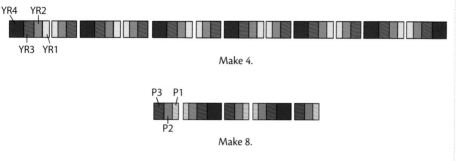

Make 4.

Make 8.

5. Stitch a purple pieced border strip to each end of each yellow pieced border strip, matching the P3 end to the YR4 fabric. Stitch pieced borders to the top and bottom of the quilt. Press toward the center. If the strips don't match the quilt center, add or remove fabric from the ends of the strips.

6. Add the P3 2½" squares to each end of the remaining pieced borders and stitch them to the sides of the quilt. Press toward the center.

• QUILT VARIATION •

Single-Star Version: Woven Logs

This version can be seen in Callie Lily *(page 62).*

The following fabric requirements and cutting instructions are for a 53" × 53" quilt. All requirements are based on 40" usable width of fabric. See General Piecing Instructions (page 5) for details on cutting methods as needed.

YARDAGE	FOR	CUTTING
Yellow to red (YR1–YR4)		
¼ yard YR1		Cut 4 strips 1⅛" wide.
¼ yard YR2		Cut 4 strips 1⅜" wide.
¼ yard YR3		Cut 4 strips 1⅝" wide.
⅓ yard YR4		Cut 4 strips 2⅛" wide.
Lavender to purple (P1–P4)		
¼ yard P1		Cut 4 strips 1⅛" wide.
¼ yard P2		Cut 4 strips 1⅜" wide.
¼ yard P3		Cut 4 strips 1⅝" wide.
¾ yard P4		Cut 4 strips 2⅛" wide
	Double-fold binding	Cut 6 strips 2¼" wide
1⅝ yards black	Diamond centers	Cut 1 strip 2½" wide. Cut one end of the strip with the ruler at a 45° angle. Subcut into 16 diamonds by measuring 2½" from that angled cut.*
	After cutting the above strip, remove the selvage from one edge of the remaining large piece and make a lengthwise cut 9" from that edge.	
	Narrow background border	From the 9"-wide piece, cut 2 strips 2" × 50½" and 2 strips 2" × 53½".**
	Setting squares and triangles	From the remaining 31"-wide piece, cut 4 squares 15¼" × 15¼" and 1 square 23" × 23". Cut the 23" square twice diagonally to yield 4 triangles.
1¾ yards 108"-wide fabric	Backing	
Batting: 61" × 61"		

*Or you can use the fast2cut Fussy Cutter 45° Diamond Guide rulers (see diagram on page 28 and Resources on page 64). **Measure your finished quilt top and adjust the border lengths as needed. These measurements are for a quilt top that measures 50½" × 50½" before borders.*

GALLERY

PRAIRIE STORM, 65" × 65", by Cheryl Meredith, quilted by Richard Weckerle, 2009

Made from the Storm at Sea diamond block.

A CHERYL M INSPIRATION, 65" × 65", by Valerie St. John, 2009

Made from the Flying Geese diamond block.

RUBIES STAR, 80" × 90", by Ruby Kosola, quilted by Cheryl Malkowski, 2009

Made from the Rolling Squares diamond block in a Rolling Star setting.

RASPBERRY DELIGHT, 54″ × 74″, by Shirley Pyle, 2009

Made from the Rolling Squares diamond and square blocks.

SWIRLING WATER, 71″ × 71″, by Pat Glass, quilted by Ramonda Weckerle, 2009

Made from the Flying Geese diamond and square blocks.

WINE COUNTRY, 86″ × 86″, by Geneva A. Croft, 2009

Made from the Woven Logs diamond and square blocks.

WINE HARVEST, 65″ × 65″, by Rene Hyland, 2009

Made from the Joseph's Coat diamond block.

BLUEBERRIES, 100″ × 100″, by Kathy Thompson,
quilted by Cheryl Meredith, 2009

Made from a smaller version of the Annie's Choice diamond block.

WHAT HAPPENED TO MY BOX?
67″ × 67″, by Judy A. Byrd, quilted
by Jane Yurk, 2009

*Made, kicking and dragging, from
the Joseph's Coat diamond block.*

MANHATTAN STAR, 53″ × 53″, by Cheryl Malkowski, 2007

Made from the New York Beauty diamond block.

MALTESE CROSS, 73″ × 73″, by Amy Vetter, 2009

Made from a smaller version of the New York Beauty diamond block.

LIKE THE WIND, 67″ × 67″,
by Cheryl Malkowski, 2009

*Made from the Flying Geese
diamond block.*

OCEAN STARBURST, 55″ × 55″, by Sharon Hager, 2009

Made from the Steps to the Altar diamond block.

HEAVEN'S RADIANT STAR, 86″ × 86″, by Joanne Sand, quilted by Richard Weckerle, 2009

Made from the New York Beauty diamond and square blocks.

GOLDEN DIAMONDS, 65″ × 65″, by Leila Dixon, quilted by Steven L. Rice of Sharon's Attic Quilt Shop, 2009

Made from the Storm at Sea diamond block.

SUNBURST, 64" × 64",
by Sarah Huie, quilted by
Debbie Foster, 2009

*Made from the Summer
Winds diamond block.*

CALLIE LILY, 53" × 53", by Lora Bateson, quilted by
Richard Weckerle, 2009

Made from the Woven Logs diamond block.

PUMPKIN SPICE, 47" × 47", by Cheryl Malkowski, 2006

Made from a smaller version of the Storm at Sea diamond block.

STAR OF ROYAL BEAUTY BRIGHT,
62″ × 62″, by Doris Koozer, 2009

Made from the Optical Illusion diamond block.

CRYSTALLINE ENTITY, 84″ × 84″, by Louise Kindig,
quilted by Cheryl Malkowski, 2008

Made from a smaller version of the Storm at Sea diamond block.

BLUE ICE SWIRL, 53″ × 53″, by Sue Muckey,
quilted by Judi Thompson, 2009

Made from the New York Beauty diamond block.

Resources

The following items make these quilts just that much more fun to create.

Add-A-Quarter ruler:
6" or 12" length

CM Designs, Inc.
7968 Kelty Tr.
Franktown, CO 80116
303-841-5920
www.addaquarter.com

fast2cut Fussy Cutter Ruler Set:
45° Diamond Guide

C&T Publishing
P.O. Box 1456
Lafayette, CA 94549
1-800-284-1114
www.ctpub.com

About the Author

Cheryl Malkowski lives in Roseburg, Oregon, with her husband and dog. She has two grown children and two grandchildren. She spends most of her time in her studio, where she designs and stitches quilts for books and fabric companies, plays on her longarm, and designs fabric. She loves to travel and teach quilt classes, and her students always take away inspiration and confidence for the tasks ahead.

Quilting since 1993, Cheryl loves all aspects of quilting except the handwork and, with determination, will find a way to do almost everything by machine. She started designing quilts in 1998 for her pattern company, cheryl rose creations, and this is her fourth book with C&T.

For more information on her lectures and workshops, for a peek into what's going on in her life, or to contact her, visit her website at www.cherylmalkowski.com or her blog at www.cherylmalkowski.com/blog.

Photo by Terry Day

Previous books by author: